THE DOMINIE WORLD OF ANIMALS

GIRAFFES

Graham Meadows & Claire Vial

Contents

DOMINIE PRESS
Pearson Learning Group

About Giraffes

The giraffe is the tallest animal in the world. An adult male can be up to eighteen feet tall and weigh as much as 3,000 pounds. Females are shorter than males and are not as heavy.

Giraffes live in the **tropical** regions of Africa. They are found mainly on grassy plains and open woodlands, where they feed on their favorite trees and grasses.

Male giraffes are called bulls. Females are called cows. Young giraffes are called calves.

Their Favorite Food

Giraffes are tall because they have long legs, large bodies, and long necks. They are able to feed on the tops of very tall trees that other animals cannot reach.

Their favorite tree is the acacia. This leafy tree has branches and twigs that are covered with sharp thorns. Because of the way giraffes eat, the thorns do not hurt them.

Their Tongues

Giraffes have very long tongues that can be up to eighteen inches in length. When a giraffe is feeding, it curls its tongue around leafy twigs and branches. Then it uses its tongue to strip off the most **nutritious** leaves.

A giraffe spends almost half of the day browsing and feeding. During that time, it eats about 75 pounds of leaves.

Their Stomachs

Giraffes eat their food quickly, without chewing it very much. Then they move to a safe place to rest.

Like cows, sheep, and goats, giraffes are **ruminants**. They have four stomachs. While they rest, they bring up small lumps of food—called cud—from their main stomach and chew it again.

Giraffes live in small groups called **herds**. A herd may contain six to twelve animals and be spread over a distance of several miles.

How They Drink

Giraffes can **extract** juices from the green leaves they eat, so they can live for two or three days without drinking water.

They cannot reach down to water just by bending their necks. In order to drink, giraffes have to spread their forelegs apart so they can lower their heads to the water's surface. This puts the giraffes in danger, because they cannot watch for other animals who might attack them.

While some giraffes are drinking, other members of the herd watch for **predators**.

Their Coats

Giraffes have a coat of brownish-yellow patches on a light background. Although all giraffes might look the same, there are several different kinds. Each type lives in a different part of Africa and can be identified by the pattern and color of patches on its coat.

The three most common varieties are the Masai giraffe, the reticulated giraffe, and the Rothschild giraffe.

Each giraffe has a **unique**, or individual, coat, just as each person has unique fingerprints.

Their Coats

The giraffe's coloring acts as a camouflage. It hides it from predators such as lions and hyenas when it is resting or out on grassy plains.

If a giraffe is attacked, its usual method of defense is to run. If a calf is too young to run fast, its mother will stand over it and defend it.

If necessary, a giraffe can deliver a deadly kick from one of its powerful legs. Few predators will risk being kicked to death.

When giraffes see a predator, they snort or **bellow** to sound an alarm.

How They Walk and Run

A giraffe has an unusual way of moving, when compared to most four-legged animals. It swings forward the front and back legs on one side of its body at the same time. This is called pacing.

When a giraffe is moving fast, or **galloping**, it curls its tail over its back and swings its long neck backward and forward to help maintain balance.

A giraffe can gallop as fast as thirty miles an hour.

Their Horns

Both male and female giraffes have a pair of bony horns, which are covered by hairy skin. Some giraffes have a second, smaller, pair of horns.

The female's horns are smaller than those of the male and have hairy **tufts** on the end. The male's horns are often bald on top, as a result of fights with other males.

Male giraffes have a small horn on their forehead between their eyes. The horn gets bigger as the giraffe grows older.

Giraffe horns can be up to five inches long.

Their Young

A baby giraffe is born while its mother is standing up, so it has a long way to drop to the ground. Once it is born, its mother licks it clean.

The calf must quickly learn how to walk; otherwise, predators such as lions and hyenas will attack it. Within a few minutes after it is born, the calf stands up on wobbly legs. Within a half-hour, it follows its mother and begins to **suckle**.

At birth, a giraffe weighs about 132 pounds and measures about six feet in height.

Their Young

After two or three weeks, the calf joins other calves in what is called a nursery group.

The young giraffe suckles its mother for about a year. It grows quickly—up to three inches a month. Giraffes live for about twenty-five years. Females are fully grown by the time they are five years old. Males can take up to three years longer to reach full growth.

When they are fully grown, giraffes are truly the tallest of all animals on earth.

The **Swahili** word for *giraffe* is *twiga*.

Glossary

bellow: To make a loud, deep noise

extract: To pull out; remove

galloping: Running very fast

herds: Groups of animals that have a common bond and live together like a family

nutritious: Healthy; nourishing; good for you

predators: Animals that hunt and kill other animals

ruminants: Animals that chew their food again after they have swallowed it

suckle: To drink a mother's milk

Swahili: A language that is spoken in many parts of East Africa

tropical: Areas that are very warm throughout the year

tufts: Small clumps, or clusters

unique: Something that is different for each person or animal

---

Index